Your Sometimes Online Life

Getting Ahead With Social Media

BY AMARA VADEE

ISBN: 1479398748
ISBN-13: 978-1479398744

DEDICATION

To the silent champions and content creators who make the
Internet a cornucopia of knowledge for all who seek it.

CONTENTS

ACKNOWLEDGMENTS

Special thanks to Genevieve DeGuzman, Debbie Brunettin, and Laura Burk. Without their help, this book wouldn't have been possible.

AMARA VADEE

CHAPTER ONE:
An Introduction

The rise of social media

Social media is an integral part of our daily lives, encompassing the tools, platforms, and software that enable individuals and groups to gather, communicate, and share information. Individuals can find love online by reviewing personal profiles on dating sites such as OkCupid and eHarmony. They can mobilize groups for social change, and even foment revolution, as was evident in Tunisia and Egypt in early 2011, with concerned citizens launching into collective action against their oppressive governments. Every day, people find various ways to stay connected to actively engage with each other. From competing with each other via socially connected games, posting an update on our personal Facebook walls, or tweeting our daily epiphanies and gripes—we are no longer just social animals but social media animals.

The golden age of social media flowered in 2006 during the rise of the so-called Web 2.0 phenomenon. It heralded the arrival of Flickr, YouTube, Myspace, Wikipedia, and the blogosphere. In Web 2.0, the Web evolved to become user-driven; a place where digital content was shared. This meant individuals could create podcasts for others to listen to, tag photos, post comments, and edit Wiki pages. In fact, bloggers joked that, "Web 2.0 is made of people!"

Social networking

One major vehicle of social media is social networking. Social networking sites and tools like Facebook, Twitter, Tumblr, Reddit, and LinkedIn have revolutionized the way people stay connected with one another. Facebook's popularity in recent years has risen to epic proportions.

Social networking has become so much a part of our lives that when you hear about China and Iran blocking certain websites in their countries indefinitely, heated discussion arises about basic human rights and freedom of speech. And, yes, you also hear about "workarounds" that some Internet users do in order just to get access, but this is often at their own personal risk and can have severe consequences.

In a day and age in which family, colleagues, and friends are scattered all over the world, and individuals socialize, collaborate, earn a living, and conduct business in the cloud, social networking has really blossomed, from something fringe and novel to a ubiquitous and daily necessity.

Risks to your privacy and personal data

With so much of our physical world being translated into the digital space, ask yourself these questions:

1. How well does your authentic self translate into your online persona (if at all)?

2. How much of yourself *should* you put out there?

3. Is there such a thing as revealing too much about yourself?

4. What information can be safely displayed or shared?

5. What do you do when the information you set free in the digital world comes back to haunt you?

With increasing demands and pressure to manage our emails, text messages, blogs, wikis, media-sharing sites, social networking sites, and virtual worlds, putting your best face forward is becoming a critical necessity when riding the social media wave. With just a few keystrokes, people can have their online presence readily available—viewable, searchable, and traceable.

Technologists and privacy experts warn that many people lack a clear grasp of the risks inherent in utilizing social media, particularly social networks. People are generally not aware who is getting access to their data, and what it will be used for.

Using social networks in conjunction with online banking and data storage tools often means surrendering some level of privacy. Indeed, the creation and linking of social network accounts (with banks, tech companies, and consumer companies, for example) makes it easier for personal details to be shared and distributed. This can be done with or without your knowledge. It is inevitable: with the erosion of privacy comes the erosion of security. As a result, your personal data can become a candy store, an easy target for criminals and other individuals with malign intents. Even low-skilled hackers can take advantage of posted information and put you at risk. With the increasing use of smartphones, e-readers, PDAs, netbooks, and laptops among consumers, the risks are even more prevalent and alarming.

Your online life may just be a small part of who you are, but it is the most public side of you out there. Here are three general risks to remember about social media and social networking in particular:

1. Staying power: What you post as a review, comment, blog or video sticks around. It is the equivalent of permanent marker on that white wall. A great deal of content stays on the Web long after the emotional high of an impulsive post.

2. Viral nature: That same review, comment, blog or video can also be shared and passed around the Web. And not only can it be replicated; it can also be modified. Remember the game "Telephone?" One whispered message at the start of the game becomes something totally different at the end. Running commentary can be copied and pasted, but also altered. For example, a polite disagreement between commentators on a blog post can potentially mutate into an ugly shouting match as communication is passed around the Internet.

3. Tracking: Trailblazing in its conceptual simplicity—

Facebook, Twitter, and other social networking sites are used by people not only to check in with one another, but also to snoop on one another. It surprised me to find that even my father—a baby boomer and retired online hobbyist—has managed to create a number of social networking profiles and been able to source some very basic information about my estranged brother with very little effort.

With these three risks in mind, the purpose of this book is to help you better grasp the importance of your digital footprint in your *sometimes* online life. Understanding the specific communication concepts behind each of the technologies will help you harness the power of communication that it offers you while staying mindful of where you leave your digital footprints. This book provides a few examples of how to take advantage of these different tools for your benefit or personal gain, but also some information on the practical safeguards.

Moving at the speed of Web is hard to do... but you do have to start somewhere!

CHAPTER TWO:
Crash Course in Social Networking and Personal Technology

Social networking: from trend to phenomenon... to

everyday tools

Social networking is no longer a one-time fad or a temporary phenomenon that will crumble with the passage of time. Sure, the effects of the recession killed the emergence of new sites and some people have become a bit jaded about keeping up to date on the latest social networking trends. Is it fair to call it social networking—or are we just hiding behind our computer screens and putting on performances that have no bearing in the real world?

For most people, social networking tools have become a means for us to share our lives with our family, friends, and colleagues, as well as the general public. Andy Warhol's famous remark, "In the future, everyone will be world-famous for 15 minutes" had amazing foresight. Think of the viral expansion of the social networking tools made available to us. It seems as if a lot of these websites were overnight successes. Our social media profiles are our portals to fame. They are essentially reality shows starring *you*. Instead of just 15 minutes of fame, the public display is continuous—or until, well, your next "update."

All around the world, people old and young check their social networking sites every day. It's an important activity in our lives that won't dissipate anytime soon. It's woven into our culture.

Social networking: why we do it

Social networking involves complex modes of self-expression. It can include a blog, a comment on Facebook or Reddit, a YouTube vlog, an Instagram photo, or a tweet. All of this content becomes part of the documentary of who you are. According to Adam Penenberg, author of *Viral Loop: From Facebook to Twitter, How Today's Smartest Businesses Grow Themselves*, we actually have three selves: a public self (the person we present to the physical world), a personal self (the person we are when alone), and the digital self (an amalgamation of the two). Of these three selves, the digital self is the most complex. For many whose social networks online exceed their social networks in real life, the digital self can be the more vivid, relevant and representative identity. In fact, scientists at the Dynamic Cognition Laboratory in Washington University in St. Louis found that when we encounter narratives, either in fiction or in a social networking medium, our brains mentally simulate the sights, sounds, movements, tastes, feelings—all the sensory and emotional experiences—as if they were real.

We are generally hardwired to socialize, and social networking is one medium of that instinctual urge to gravitate toward communities and collaboration. It explains our desire to "friend" people who ask send us invitations on Facebook, or our need to keep up with a steady stream of tweets and blogs. Technology enables us to strengthen social ties by responding to messages faster and more efficiently. While nothing takes the place of face-to-face contact, physical interactions can sometimes be limited or inconvenient. It doesn't matter who you are (someone working overseas, a soldier assigned to Iraq or Afghanistan, a stay-at-home parent sharing recipes with other parents, an entrepreneur trying to widen your business networks)—social networking provides us with a way to bridge distances.

Social media was initially designed to connect people, so it's no surprise that most of us use it for personal reasons. Staying connected with old friends, coworkers and family can be fun and exciting. It is a cheaper way to keep in touch, and is much faster than sending snail mail. With the advent of video calls, texting, and tweeting, you can now keep up with your friends and family in real time. However, if you determine that you want to use social media for personal purposes, there are many guidelines and safeguards you should be aware of, for protecting yourself online.

Using social media and technology to introduce yourself, connect with or maintain relationships with business contacts is a great way to keep up with your budding network. Whether you are in the market for employment, looking to expand your business, or seeking to project a particular kind of image, using social media and technology can be incredibly efficient. However, it is not a substitute for real-life interpersonal communication.

Social media sites inarguably help pave the way for offline gatherings. These social gatherings help cement relationships—professional or otherwise—establish connections, and of course put a real face behind an avatar or a handle. Indeed, marketing strategists are no longer limited to traditional media. Social media has been crucial in marketing endeavors.

As interaction shifts seamlessly between personal interaction and digital interaction, the tools and widgets you use in order to share this world become extremely important. This content can take on a life of its own. Like a series of mirrors turned inward, the information replicates and expands, moving from your network to your friends' networks, and throughout their personal and professional networks.

The risks of social networking

All this has stirred something of a collective identity crisis and stimulated heated debate in social and legal circles about the measures to protect individual identity.

The consequences are real. For instance, Virgin Atlantic Airways took disciplinary action against a group of crew members who participated in a Facebook discussion that insulted passengers and criticized the airline's safety standards. A high-school teacher in Georgia was reprimanded by her school district and forced to resign over photos on her Facebook page depicting her holding a glass of wine and a beer. A college senior in Pennsylvania was forced to forfeit her teaching credentials when she criticized her supervisor on her Myspace page. The case drew national attention when she sued the university in federal court and lost. The court ruled that there was no First Amendment violation because her Myspace postings were not issues of public concern, but "Personal matters."

Facebook often revises their privacy policy to require users to take action if they wish to keep information private, making most of that information public by default. Most personal data is now being shared with third-party websites while you browse the Web.

While many advocates and regulators want to push for measures that would make it easier for people to erase their digital mistakes (including a range of options to make parts of our digital footprint disappear) the goal of being able to reconstruct our virtual identities is still a long way off. Once a part of ourselves is made public in the digital realm, it is very difficult to erase it. Your best bet is to take preventative measures.

Social, anthropological, and even legal debates aside, what we do know is that social media, and social networking in particular, is an inextricable part of our lives—and at the very least we should learn how to manage it and become more circumspect and careful in how we approach our digital lives.

Instead of focusing on privacy controls, I'd like to introduce the philosophy that when you put any information online, it is not private. The moment the information leaves your fingertips, it is open to the public to view, consume, and document. No privacy policy, control settings, or moderation will be able to save your content from itself.

Not just for socializing: other uses for social networking

Some people erroneously think of social networking only as a phenomenon. Social media includes a series of tools and outlets for social networking. We generally participate in social networking to accomplish something, plan events, mobilize a movement, draw attention to a cause, track down old friends, publicize our professional experiences for a prospective employer, cultivate a professional network, and share or seek information. The uses are varied. Social networking as a means to an end is very powerful. It determines whether it is used as an attention waster (like flipping channels on the TV) or whether you can use it to advance some personal or professional objective. In fact, putting these tools together in an environment that encourages community and collaboration has enormous potential for doing good and achieving a wide range of goals.

Social networking is no longer the exclusive domain of college students and teens looking to check each other out and socialize. The demographics of users are more pervasive and widespread. Here's a sampling of social-networking-savvy groups you might have not expected:

1. *For businesses and entrepreneurs.* More than any other technology, social networking exemplifies the trend toward the consumerization of information technology. Businesses are increasingly leveraging social media platforms such as Facebook to create a ready consumer fan base to expand their marketing and contribute to research.

2. *Large-scale companies.* Businesses are also using social networking tools to recruit prospective employees and to headhunt for executives and professionals. LinkedIn, a popular online business network, houses a database of professionals and has become popular in recent years in serving companies'

staffing needs and providing professionals with a platform to network and seek out professional collaboration.

3.   Up-and-coming artists, investors, and otherwise inspired citizens have employed crowdfunding tools to fuel their passions. Crowdfunding sites such as Kickstarter.com and Indiegogo.com use crowd participation and viral enthusiasm to fundraise from virtual strangers for specific projects. Funders can browse profiles of people and their projects and contribute various amounts. Nowadays anyone can be an angel investor. Etsy.com is a virtual marketplace where people can browse and sell homemade items, from artisanal cookies to necklaces and earrings, as well as original art.

4.   *For parents and grandparents.* Baby boomers are one of the active demographics on social networking sites. They are recently divorced parents connecting with old high-school flames, empty nesters planning group outings, and retirees looking to organize book clubs. According to a Pew Research Center Internet study, one-third of adults have a profile on a social networking site, a spike from

eight percent in 2005. The older set was traditionally slow to embrace the technology, but that has changed. Adults aged 65 and older, followed by those aged 50 to 64, are the fastest-growing group of social networking site users, according to the Pew Research Center.

5.   *Politicos and social movement groups.* The height of political engagement on social networks occurred during the 2012 presidential election. The Obama camp mobilized millions through a Facebook campaign, utilized YouTube and Twitter to ignite energy among constituents, attract voter attention, and fuel a political momentum that kept him in the White House. In contrast to 2008 in which Democrats used online social networks to incite their base, 2010 saw Republican voters and Tea Party supporters using these outlets to get their messages out. Social networking connects others with similar political, social and religious ideologies.

6.   *Do-gooders and the socially conscious.* Social networking is often used to bridge together fundraisers and organizations. For example, Crowdrise.com is a platform that connects social networking accounts to

virtual fundraising pages that allow people to spread the word about causes and non-profits they care about, while at the same time raising money. The idea is to leverage the goodwill of people all across the world to help nonprofits achieve their missions, in a targeted, project-specific way. With the help of social media experts in various fields, nonprofits can scale up, plus they have access to a pool of experts they would not have reached before. This is not simply advertising for volunteers to fill soup bowls at the soup kitchen; rather it is fundraising at a larger level—only made possible by this level of social networking.

CHAPTER THREE:
Know the Key Tools of Social Media

Nuts and bolts of social networking

Just like many things in life, social media is not a "One size fits all" solution. You must carefully determine your objective before deciding which social networking tool will best represent your interests. Before you start blazing through the social media sites, there are a few basic elements that you should set up prior to developing your profiles:

1. **Your own personal email.** This can end with @hotmail.com, @yahoo.com or @gmail.com, but a domain that is registered in your name is actually preferred. It can be any domain name of your choosing—your name or otherwise—but it should always be appropriate in every setting. (It is best to choose an email that you can use for both personal and

professional purposes.)

2. **Your own blog.** Whether you use it for professional or personal purposes, having an Internet footprint that you can maintain on your own is very important. Think of it as a credit card. People won't trust you with their money if you have not established your "good credit" history. Same thing with a blog or your own site. It is a validation of your existence.

3. **Your tagline.** It should be short (less than eight words), insightful and descriptive, yet alluring enough to entice readers to learn more about you.

4. **Your bio.** It should be well written, in the third person, and include some vital professional stats. This is your chance to start with a clean slate so choose the highlights of your career and resist the temptation to copy-paste your whole curriculum vitae (unless you are actually putting up a site for your CV). A long self-congratulatory bio can be pretty boring to read.

After you have those things prepared, you are all set to make your digital social debut!

You can make social media and technology work in your favor if you know how to use it wisely. Learning to distinguish between different potential uses of each website is the important first step in learning about how to manage them. Social media can be many things, but first and foremost you must determine how it is supposed to serve the ultimate end user: YOU.

So, how do you tame these beasts? That's simple: Get to know them first.

Some social networks we hear about are fly-by-night startups that rarely make it past one fiscal year. By the time we wrap our brains around these social networking sites, the trends blow over and everyone has moved on to the next hot thing (and you are left with several inactive accounts in the digital netherworld). From peer-to-peer sites to blogs and online communities, social media has flourished over the last decade and will most likely consume an even larger portion of our online lives in the coming future.

Despite the sheer volume of social media outlets that crop up daily, there are a few staples that you have probably already heard of: Facebook, Twitter, LinkedIn, and WordPress. Because of the volume of users and the way each of these social networks has revolutionized the communications process, the text will focus the discussion on these particular websites.

Facebook

Among the handful of social networking sites available on the Internet, Facebook is the household name, the de facto platform through which citizens of the world connect. Users can create a personal profile page to connect with family members, add other users as "friends," and exchange messages. Users can also join common-interest groups categorized according to various characteristics.

While Google helps us find data and information, and YouTube keeps us entertained and informed, Facebook really aims to do something even simpler. Facebook encourages us to broadcast our lives online. We smile, laugh, look goofy or cool in photos we later post on Facebook. We post witty comments in hopes that someone will notice and respond.

Think Facebook is just a social networking site? Think again. Facebook also drives Web traffic globally. On a monthly basis, hundreds of millions of people engage with Facebook via Facebook Connect, a one-click sign-on button on various websites. Instead of creating a separate account on that site, users can log in using their Facebook credentials. Even Myspace, its one-time rival, has announced that it is partnering with Facebook on Facebook Connect. The logic is simple: Facebook credentials lure people who haven't yet created an account or opt not to. Facebook drives Web traffic.

Facebook also continues to grow and make connections through businesses. Think about the "Like" button. A million likes on a topic or trend is a million points of data to help companies package and sell products and services. Facebook also has something else that helps businesses: the power of peer pressure. We are all more likely to try something or buy a product that our friends like.

This section will address the differences between having a "FREE" account and renting out your information. A lot of people don't realize that they give up a certain amount of rights when they seek free services/information online. Your account is free at the expense of your privacy.

Get the most out of Facebook:

1. *Add content from other sources using RSS or*

NetworkedBlogs. If you create your own content on YouTube, WordPress, and Twitter, there are ways for you to publish those updates on Facebook. It is an easy way to keep all of your accounts in sync while providing your friends with the most up-to-date information about what's going on in your world.

2. *Add photos:* Specialist photo sites (like Flickr) or video sites (like Vimeo) can be seamlessly integrated into Facebook. Photos in Flickr, for example, can be exported directly to Facebook's photo albums. Mac users can conduct bulk photo exports from iPhoto to Facebook. Facebook uses an "infinite scroll" feature that enables you to browse photos faster.

3. *Use wall posts to share information:* Each Facebook account/profile has a "wall" that functions like a chalkboard on which users can post messages, comments, links, videos, and photos.

4. *Update your Status regularly:* Your Facebook profile enables you to publish a "status" of yourself for friends in your network to read.

5. *Update your Profile regularly.* Facebook is always

evolving new ways to share moments and information about your life, particularly interests and activities. Users can list the projects they worked on at a job, classes being taken in school, favorite musicians, sports teams, and others. Interests and experiences are now represented by images, which makes for a more compelling and vivid profile.

6. *Check out how you connect with your networks:* List your schools, companies you've worked for, and charities you've volunteered at. When you visit another user's profile, it will show you all you have in common, such as mutual friends, events you're both attending, shared photos, wall posts, and shared groups. It'll also help build exposure for you.

Twitter

Twitter is essentially a broadcasting service that enables users to send and read *tweets*, which are short text-based messages. These tweets are publicly visible but can be restricted to only a few select people known as "followers." Users can subscribe to other users' Twitter pages and become followers. As a follower, you can view the tweets displayed in reverse chronological order on your main

Twitter page, seeing a mix of tweets scrolling down the page like a newsfeed.

Twitter is a different sort of social networking tool than Facebook. Its users are from all walks of life. Celebrities, politicians, actors, musicians, bloggers, and news organizations are using Twitter to make announcements and proclamations. This rapid growth has attracted some criticism as many deride it as a time-waster. In 2009, Twitter gained credence when it played a role in the disputed Iranian elections, helping organize protests and disseminating information. The State Department even contacted Twitter and requested a delay on the network's scheduled maintenance to allow service to continue and thus keep Iranians and interested parties swapping and exchanging information about the elections.

Like it or not, tweets are becoming a part of history. In 2010, the Library of Congress, the 210-year-old bastion of human knowledge, announced that it would digitally house every public tweet ever made since Twitter's inception in 2006. The mass of tweets would number in the billions and represent an attempt to archive the musings of everyday people. The library's director of communications, Matt Raymond, has extolled Twitter's "Immense impact on culture and history," citing it as the communication tool of choice for many public figures, including Barack Obama who used it to declare victory in the 2012 elections, and protestors in Egypt's uprising who used it to topple its authoritarian government. Will knowing that the Library of Congress is preserving tweets for posterity alter user habits?

Get the most out of Twitter:

1. *Use Twitter to find real-time information.* Twitter's search tool is incredibly helpful in finding up-to-the-second information. For example, if the your cell phone service goes down, and you want to find out why, hop on Twitter and see what people are saying about your service. The same goes for checking traffic updates, reading movie reviews, finding out the outcome of a much-beloved TV show, and so much more. Depending on where you live, you might even be able to tap into a neighborhood crime blotter! Provided you have enough followers (with enough knowledge), Twitter can be a great forum for asking questions and getting answers.

2. *Use Twitter to monitor issues, trends, products, and events important to you.* Twitter is essentially a newsfeed

and so it is the easiest way to stay up to date on the latest developments and news about the things you love and the things you hate. There are several Twitter client apps that let you create a particular Twitter search feed, and keep track of whatever you want.

3. *Use Twitter to communicate with your social network.* That's easy. Twitter is meant to keep people connected with their friends and family. Twitter can be an effective communication tool if your tweets are well thought out. You can use it to connect with people professionally as well, so put in extra care to truly connect with people.

4. *Use Twitter to boost productivity.* Twitter's geotagged tweets, which enable users to connect an update with a location, provide a real-time newsfeed view of what's happening on the spot in any particular place and at any particular time. Twitter can also be connected with your other social networks.

LinkedIn

LinkedIn is a global professional network with millions of members. LinkedIn serves as your own personal portfolio of trusted contacts with whom you can connect and explore professional opportunities within a broad network. Think of LinkedIn as a Facebook for your career.

If a career in social media is your ultimate goal, getting on LinkedIn is an absolute must. Any company that has a social media presence will be on LinkedIn. To convey your professionalism, you will need to have a fleshed-out profile with up-to-date information about your abilities, connections, recommendations, endorsements, and more.

Get the most out of LinkedIn:

1. *Scope out the competition or follow companies:* You can track and monitor what others in your industry are doing, see the groups people have joined, or find out when your contacts have switched jobs. You can also "follow" companies and organizations you want to target.

2. *Use the Introductions feature:* Ask your Connections if you can be introduced to others in companies you want to target or reach.

3. *Get LinkedIn recommendations from your Connections.* Nothing catapults your LinkedIn profile more than strong

recommendations from your colleagues, former managers, and fellow employees. Use LinkedIn to ask your Connections to make recommendations and endorsements. These kudos will be displayed on your profile page for prospective clients or employers to see.

4. *Find out where people with similar backgrounds are working:* Conduct a search of users with your skills, within a specific ZIP code you want to be in. For example, if you're a programmer who wants to move to San Francisco, search for profiles with that zip code and use keywords that highlight your skill set (e.g. JavaScript, PHP, Rails, etc.).

5. *Track other people's mobility within the industry:* Say you're working for Company X or interested in Company Y. Using LinkedIn's "Company Profiles," you can easily track where current employees worked and where employees out the door are headed. Company pages also list "New Hires"—LinkedIn users hired by the company—which can be useful in checking out the backgrounds of recently hired employees. That information may help inform you of their talent pool and what it takes to get your foot in the door.

WordPress

WordPress is a powerful publishing platform that allows you to create your own website and blog fairly quickly and easily. WordPress also offers users access to a toolkit of analytics and built-in networking. Mimicking Facebook, WordPress also offers a "Like" button for users to emphasize the content they prefer and share it with their network co-members as well as their Facebook friends. It is one of the single most powerful tools available to you right now and it's absolutely free.

Get the most out of WordPress:

1. *Use WordPress to generate feedback for an idea or product.* Many users use WordPress to gather feedback from customers. WordPress blogs can give users a place to voice their opinions and provide feedback, which can provide instant market research and keep your most loyal clients and fans happy.

2. *Use WordPress to establish a dialogue.* Spark conversations between you and your customers, and between your customers and each other. Connect your community members with each other through discussion,

whether or not it directly relates to your company. This strengthens the community and instills loyalty between the members.

3. *Use WordPress to provide quality content and media for your social network.* WordPress supports photos, videos, blog posts, events, and other types of content—so take advantage and encourage your community to submit their own content as well.

4. *Use WordPress to promote your work.* WordPress makes it easy to share a lot of different types of content. The possibilities are endless.

Dealing with the "Goldilocks Dilemma"

With the wealth of social networking sites out there, including the popular ones just discussed, social media has made greater strides than we ever dreamed possible when the Web was just a collection of websites and blogs. Interactions have become more sophisticated and nuanced. This raises many questions about the numerous privacy issues on protecting valuable connections from prying eyes, exploitation from unethical marketers, and cyber assaults from criminal hackers.

Faced with so many tools and uses, we have essentially a "Goldilocks Dilemma." We have so many tools, and if we share too much information, that information can become a paradise of easy pickings for marketers. However, if we share too little, we end up losing the spirit of what makes social networking so powerful: communication with others, networking (in the old-fashioned sense), and reaching a wider audience. The amount of information shared has to be just right.

CHAPTER FOUR:
Your Digital Footprint –
Promote But Protect Yourself

Does social networking mean the end of privacy?

We now live in an information age where huge parts of our lives and the economy depend on information. Social media is very much about the technologies we use to shuttle and move this information around; it is an enabler for our social relations. What we sometimes forget is that the information that fuels the social media economy is *our information.* It's personal information about us.

I use Facebook pretty often—sometimes to waste time, but most of the time to do something useful. I use it to stay in touch with extended family who live all over the world: I can see what they did yesterday, what events they are planning to attend, what they are thinking, and so forth. I also use it to fundraise for non-profit organizations and to syndicate my blog; and when I was consulting for other companies, I used it to demonstrate my social media prowess.

Social networking sites give us access to intimate details that enrich our relationships in the real world, as if no distance were separating us. The same is true about my work. Social networks like LinkedIn help me "network" in a natural, nonaggressive manner. More than once I have contacted sources through a social network. It is a useful jumping-off point to make business deals, find old buddies, research a job lead, and more.

Contrary to the belief among social media skeptics, social networking does not foster antisocial behavior. Making virtual connections on a social networking site does not cripple our ability to connect with people in the real world. In my opinion, it is in fact the *reliance* on such technology that hinders our ability to make meaningful connections in person.

Clive Thompson, a social media writer, has explored this phenomenon and likens it to what social scientists call "ambient awareness." For example, when we log on to Facebook, or check Twitter, we are bombarded with succinct bits of information about people that eventually add up to the broad outlines of someone's life, providing a rich opportunity for deeper conversation in the next meet-up.

Steven Johnson, author of *Where Good Ideas Come From* also praises the notion of going public as a civic good. While there are some social media users who will shamelessly indulge in idle voyeurism and egotism, there are many more who have used social networking tools to make the world a richer place. He cites how several close friends have blogged their way through battles with cancer and other illnesses, unintentionally fostering a community among fellow sufferers undergoing the same ordeals. They were able to receive unsolicited advice and support in the form of comments and tweets—a trove of amassed knowledge that others looking for answers could also access. Johnson calls this a lesson in the "Virtues of public-ness"—oversharing can lead to civic returns.

But social media also touches on aspects of privacy in our lives that are not so clear-cut.

They often say that everyone in the world is connected by no more than six degrees of separation. Facebook, LinkedIn, and the plethora of social media properties build their businesses based on that notion. We have learned to use social networking to create a web of friends, families, colleagues and business contacts. This has led to an interesting phenomenon—an extension of our daily lives into a digital one. In the days before social media, celebrity was the only cause for gossip and notoriety. Now anyone can expect this level of scrutiny, once the privilege of just the famous and infamous.

Social media is definitely a catalyst for a lot of good and transparency—but we are only at the tip of the iceberg when it comes to understanding the costs of sharing even the most mundane details about our lives. Welcome to the digital age, where we seemingly have the option to reinvent ourselves and start anew, or change our identities—at least our digital selves. But do we really?

Mark Zuckerberg, the founder of Facebook, made the grand proclamation: "I would expect that next year, people will share twice as much information as they share this year, and next year, they will be sharing twice as much as they did the year before." Companies like Facebook depend on the willingness of their users to share. The more personal information a social networking site collects, the more attractive the site becomes to potential advertisers and the more revenue it can generate. So safeguards are not in the best interests of social networking companies.

Mary Madden, a senior researcher at the Pew Research Center and head of the Pew Internet Project, has cautioned that, "Social networking requires vigilance, not only in what you post, but what your friends post about you... Now you are responsible for everything."

Getting your digital footprint right

In the realm of social media, the speed of delivering and receiving juicy tidbits has become lightning fast. Distance is no longer an issue, nor is time (sometimes). Digital media is dissemination at the speed of now. With the age of technology comes a massive data trail that even the beginner Internet user leaves behind quickly and deeply. This means that your information can be generated on your cell phone, computer, social networking profiles, and with general Internet access locations.

A Pew Research Center Internet study shows that 60% of those who search for their names actually find information about themselves online, but 38% say their searches come up short. On those who found information about themselves, 11% found the data to be inaccurate while 4% cited that the information about them online was downright embarrassing. The same study shows the most common information people may find when searching for you:

1. 72% - contact information

2. 37% - professional accomplishments or interests

3. 33% - profile on a social and professional networking site

4. 31% - images

5. 31% - public records

6. 28% - personal background information.

We are social beings and no matter what you do, people will continue to nose around your business. You might as well provide them with factually accurate information. It is recommended that you maintain some type of profile online, even if all of them are set to private. It is better to register all of the key social networking sites in your name before someone else tries to register it and then uses it to take advantage of you.

When the call was made to minimize carbon footprint, everyone started going digital. Yet here, too, we are trying to find ways to minimize our digital footprints. Your active participation on the Web and social media sites fuels the amount of information you put in. It is your job to keep the information you distribute fairly accurate and it is also your responsibility to guard yourself from digital threats.

Minimizing threats to your digital footprint

Want to live off the grid and minimize your digital trail? That's going to be very difficult, given the infrastructure of the Web:

1. When you sign in to your account to read your news online, you give the newspaper or magazine permission to keep track of your viewing habits—what articles you read and what advertisements you click on.

2. When you check your personal email at work during down time, management may be using spyware to track your activities. The National Security Agency can monitor all emails without a warrant and without informing you.

3. When you buy a book online, the company keeps track of your purchases, knowing what you've browsed, previous purchases made, and shipping addresses.

4. Visit a café with free Wi-Fi and have your IP address logged and recorded, and risk being accosted by hackers and fraudsters wandering the wired connection.

You're not a digital hermit, but you want to stay safe. Here are some basic tips for minimizing your digital footprint:

1. *Don't feed the Cookie Monster.* The HTTP cookie, Web browser cookie, or just cookie for short can be used for authentication or storing site data or preferences. A cookie is not bad in itself as it helps facilitate smooth browsing activities. Allowing cookies to persist between browsing sessions often lets you skip the login step for entering a site. An alternative approach is to configure your browser to clear all cookies when you exit or close the browser, which ensures that other sites won't harvest the cookies.

2. Your cache may be growing a monster right this very minute. Delete your cookies and opt for private browsing from your Internet tools. This way, every time you close your browser, any data stored will be deleted.

3. *Keep two email addresses.* Keep one email address for your official transactions such as keeping correspondence, and another for sites you are not familiar with.

4. *Do not open email attachments from unknown senders.* Files from email attachments are known to carry malware, adware, and spyware.

5. *Update your security patches and fixes.* Your computer usually prompts you for security patches every now and then. Make it a habit to check for this. Give your laptop or computer a regular health check.

6. *Lock up as you go.* Sign out or log out whenever you're done browsing a site that requires your username and password. You don't leave your empty house unlocked do you? Your personal information is your property. Keep it safe.

7. *Exercise your neurons.* It is so much easier to click on the "Keep me logged in" or "Remember my session" checkbox so you don't have to recall your password next time you browse the site. However, doing so puts your account information within easy reach of would-be hackers. The reason you forget passwords is precisely because you don't

use much of the "memory" part of your brain function. Use it. It'll keep you mentally healthy and your digital information safe.

Defensive networking: what you need to know about privacy settings

So you say you have 600 Facebook friends and 1,200 followers on Twitter? Are they really all your friends? Know that not everyone is your real friend or even has your best interests in mind. Even real friends can become enemies. Not to mention the other friends you've reeled in.

In the blogosphere, I know of a blogger who thought that only her family and friends were reading her blog. But once her site was tweeted and shared over and over, she was put in the spotlight—just like that, from one viewer (probably her mom) to thousands! And all of a sudden, she realized that her blog wasn't for public consumption. She tried to change the privacy settings, but the blog had already been read, screen-captured, posted, reposted, and talked about many times over. It was simply too late.

Just remember that what you publish on social media sites is public and will be there for everyone to see. The Internet collects all kinds of information and deleting it can be difficult.

Defensive networking is very much like defensive driving. Networking online with people you already know (or strangers) can be fun if done right, but not every relationship ends with a "happily ever after." Being defensive in your online networking means disclosing personal information only to those you trust. Defensive networking also means that you connect only with those who have verified identities and positive intentions.

Defensive networking also means that if you have a falling out with someone, you "de-friend" them online immediately. Do not wait for time to cool down or for the issues to simmer. You want to get rid of all ties and sever them as quickly as possible. If you maintain even distant connections with them, they may use the information you post against you. And don't be so quick to forgive. Just like in the real world, let that someone earn your trust first before adding them to your friend list again. A human can forget— but unfortunately the Web does not forget easily.

Privacy settings

While we can be naturally protective of our privacy, we also enjoy asserting our identity, expressing ourselves, and broadcasting our lives to the world, whether to incite joy, cheap laughs, admiration, or a host of other communal emotions. There is a way to cope with this duality in our natures as social media animals in the realm of social networking: the privacy setting.

Our profiles on social networks like Facebook are oftentimes freewheeling and joyful online confessionals of our everyday lives. How do we feel about letting a third party become the gatekeepers of our information? I can't emphasize the importance of knowing the privacy policies of all the social networking sites you work on. Get to learn and love them. They are different for every social networking outlet and are constantly updated. Spending time tinkering with your privacy settings can do you a world of good. Most of the social networking sites that are widely available to you are initially set to be a completely public, indexable Web presence. Knowing this from the outset will help guide your decisions as to exactly how private you want to be. Don't be too intimidated by the list of checkboxes you have to go through. They are actually written in easy-to-understand terms. And if in doubt, ask someone for help.

Here are the links to enable you to directly manage your privacy settings on a few of today's popular social networking sites:

1. Facebook:

   http://www.facebook.com/settings/?tab=privacy

2. Twitter: http://twitter.com/settings/account

3. LinkedIn: https://www.linkedin.com/secure/settings

4. YouTube:

   http://www.youtube.com/account#privacy/search

Defensive social networking: the best self-defense

Facebook is particularly notorious for its privacy settings and deserves extra mention. Facebook's information philosophy is that sharing is good. They encourage users to share almost everything that is included in their Facebook accounts, which means that if you open an account for the first time or have never made any changes to your privacy settings, your Facebook profile is an open book—not only to your friends and groups on the site, but everyone across the entire network.

Have you ever wondered what information financial institutions ask for in order to reset accounts? It is often data that could be found on your social networking profile and exploited if you're not careful: birth date, residence, email address.

Your very own Facebook account gives strangers ready access to your sensitive information that could easily enable criminals and fraudsters to impersonate you and steal your identity.

Here are some general tips to keep in mind when practicing defensive social networking:

1. *Use the block.* You should have different levels of "openness" with everyone in your social network. Try classifying members: close friends (full disclosure of your profile), work colleagues, acquaintances, family, etc. You can be as refined and detailed as you want in these categorizations. Once someone is part of your social network, they will have different levels of access to information, based on their relationship to you. Ask yourself, do you want everyone you went to college with to see your photos, or just your close buddies? Customize the access to your information. What do you do if your boss wants to add you to his/her network? Rather than reject the invitation (potentially a career-crushing move), accept the request and slap an information block on your profile— especially that photo album titled "Best Party Moments of 2010."

2. *Cull your social network.* Tidy up your network by doing a regular social network purge. It sounds harsh, but is very useful. Go through the member lists and reduce them down to more manageable numbers. Too many friends (in this case, members that are more like strangers) can also clog your news feed if you're generous with every invitation you receive. Be aware of promiscuous social networking before it turns into full-blown situations of awkward moments and paranoia. That said, there are times when adding strangers to your social network can be permissible—that's part of the fun of the technology—just stay alert and exercise caution.

3. *When it comes to privacy settings, do a clean sweep.* A clean sweep means disabling all of the options and then opening them one by one. Add the bells and whistles—social networking options and features you want—rather than having to subtract them, in order to avoid missing any gaping security holes and to ensure you start with everything accessible.

4. *Give yourself a background check.* Take a few minutes to scour the Web for dirt on yourself. This is absolutely

crucial. Get to know what's out there on the World Wide Web with your name and you'll be able to better determine what steps you need to take to build (or fix) your online reputation. You might have written something a long time ago that isn't true now (like your perfect vital statistics 15 summers ago) and would like to take it down. This is the perfect opportunity to do so. Here are a few major places you should be checking:

Google.com

Bing.com

Ask.com

Dogpile.com

LinkedIn.com

Facebook.com

Twitter.com

Zoominfo.com

Names.whitepages.com

Think before you click/share/post

Information is power. Remember that those tiny bits of information about yourself can help build you up as a person and as an online entity, but can also be abused and used against you. How much information are you willing to divulge? Should we be comfortable revealing details and facets of our lives on the Web: Favorite foods? Number of sexual partners? We are known as the tell-all generation—but when should we be living out loud and when should we be keeping our personal lives private?

Posting comments or sharing information on public forums

Are you mad at your boss? Looking to blow off some steam by typing a string of expletives into a blog? Reposting a racy joke onto Twitter? How about posting your favorite place to put your purse in your status feed on Facebook? (Naughty guys and gals—you know who you are!)

You might want to think twice before you click on "Post" or "Share." I have general rules of thumb that I use before I post any sort of information on a public forum:

1. *How would my family feel about my post?* Look at your post from the eyes of your audience, and, more importantly, your family. Your friends may understand your post, but will your family?

2. *Ten years from now, what will this post say about me?* What you put out there in the digital fabric can last forever. Scandalous videos can live on long after the gossip has died down. Will your posted video, comment or blog come back to haunt you?

3. *What would a potential employer think about this?* Some employers take time to check your online persona. There was even an instance when an employer I knew lost interest in an applicant just because of her choice of email address (think "cuteandcuddly@yahoo.com"). The email address just didn't exude professionalism and this impacts how you are judged. Another incident was when an employer was calling an applicant and the ringback tone was that of a theme from a horror movie. The applicant ended up scaring the job away.

4. *How does this reflect on my character?* What you post says a lot about you as a person. Are you revealing your

authentic self online or channeling some fictional character? Either way, are you leaving your audience with the right impression?

5. *Will I damage anyone else's reputation with this?* Are you disclosing another's information? Or posting something that may be taken out of context? Read, edit, reread, and re-edit before you commit to what you're going to share. Last time I checked, slander is still a crime that can land you in court.

6. *If you are reposting information, is it informative or slanderous?* When an earthquake hit Haiti in 2010, social networking helped in a big way to spread the news and updates. Posting and reposting through Twitter and Facebook helped source donations and mobilize rescue missions. These kinds of messages are not only informative but helpful as well. But recycling information can also have negative effects, particularly if the information is negative. Exercise caution and avoid contributing to a "chain-mail effect" for disparaging or malicious information.

7. *Are you comfortable sharing this information?* Overall, you have to listen to your gut feelings. If you feel

comfortable about sharing that piece of yourself on the Web, then by all means, share it! But if there's even an ounce of doubt nagging inside of you, you might want to edit what you're about to say. Better yet, don't share at all.

I would advise you to take into careful thought and consideration everything you put out into the digital universe. Any of these bytes of information can come back and haunt you. Spew wisely.

Before hitting "Send..."

Social media fiends are a clicker-happy bunch. Posting information in the digital realm has sort of become a sport. If you're always in a hurry, sooner or later you will find yourself in a quandary.

Have you ever sent an email hastily and found yourself clicking on the "cancel" button relentlessly because you just sent it to the wrong person? Or tried retrieving the email you just sent, but to no avail? In our day-to-day life, whether in the workplace or at home, everything is fast-paced and everyone seems to be in a rush all the time. It's the same for our online lives! Have you ever noticed that while rereading a message you're about to send via email, your pointer is already hovering impatiently over the "send" button? Worse, you didn't even have time to check your message, and you just hit "send."

The thing about social media is that whenever you make a statement or send an offensive email, you leave behind a digital footprint that is forever archived. Deleting email, tweets or offensive Facebook wall posts don't automatically erase it from the minds of the people who have read it. Unfortunately, information is published at the speed of light with the Internet. Learn to communicate responsibly and to exercise caution before you post any bit of information online. Responsible communication means understanding the ramifications of the information you post or leak long before you actually do it.

Remember that effective communication requires you to craft your messages correctly with the recipient in mind. There are different ways of composing a message for different people. Understanding that you only have fractions of a second to make the best first impression, make sure you are getting your message across and check (and recheck) that you've actually chosen the recipient correctly.

Consider the following elements before you hit send:

1. *Posting your location.* Although it might be fun to use apps such as Foursquare to simply to track your whereabouts, it may not be the safest bet. Ladies especially be forewarned that location-tracking applications make it easy for people to prey on you, whether you are alone or not. It is best to be on the cautious side, but if you must participate in location-tracking activities please only allow close friends and family to access that information.

2. Women are not the only vulnerable targets. In January 2011, there was a case in the UK where a 22-year-old woman stalked a man using Foursquare. The woman would use the information gleaned from Foursquare to harass him, barraging him with nasty messages. Ultimately, the incident worsened, forcing the man to cease using Foursquare and to close both his Twitter and Facebook accounts as well.

3. Any information that is publicly accessible makes it incredibly easy for anyone to track your whereabouts, and that compromises your safety.

4. *Posting your emotions.* Angry at your boss? Annoyed with the chairman of the board? Let off some steam on some of

your social media profiles and that could backfire—quickly. Most new hires are pretty good at separating their work life from their online private life. Unfortunately, if you've been around for a month or two, you've probably gotten comfortable at work and started befriending some of your coworkers. That means that when you start airing your grievances online to what you believe are your "friends" you are actually putting your foot in your mouth and giving potential enemies ammunition with which to smear your good name. This reminds me of an employee who, after being berated at work, sent an SMS to a coworker complaining about his boss, complete with a string of expletives. He found himself out of work the very next day because he actually sent the SMS to his boss.

5. Remember the principle, "Praise in public—reprimand in private." It's something you might want to apply to your online life as well.

6. *Posting your opinions.* Have a political or religious statement you want to make? It's probably best to relegate those opinions to their appropriate forums and secret diaries. Writing dissertation-like wall posts may not bode

well for your professional image—unless, of course, you are pursuing a career as a pundit or a radical. Although opinions are great to have, they add to the online noise that distracts people from your best side, painting a skewed picture of you. It is perfectly acceptable to post your perspective on an issue or to weigh in on a current event. It is another thing to post heated, poorly crafted arguments.

7. *Posting your secrets.* Well, obviously, if it's a secret, then why post it? Some things are better left unsaid. If you really need to vent in the digital arena, start a blog with a secret email address and make no reference to your name and location and post it there. That way you always have a place to vent your frustrations and post your secrets but don't compromise your online identity. Some websites like Postsecret.com have made it their mission to be a venue for those who want to reveal their secrets creatively without revealing their identities.

8. Also, it doesn't matter if you post it online in a public forum like Facebook or email it to a trusted confidante— leaving any digital footprint of a secret is never a good idea.

9. *Posting proprietary information.* If you are a new hire at

work, you might have been asked to sign a non-disclosure agreement. Even if not, sometimes you may be working on projects that are otherwise classified for the world at large. Maybe your firm just landed some new business that they needed to keep under wraps. Maybe your company is doing some damage control from some bad press. Giving a minute-by-minute status update via your personal social media profiles is not only unethical but opens you up to some pretty serious liability issues.

10. *Reply vs. Reply All – know the difference.* Replying to one person is very different from replying to all. It completely changes the dynamic of the communications when you know that everyone else is watching. On work communications, it is generally best to reply to all when a threaded email discussion and teamwork are necessary.

Taking precaution with your essentials

I have a friend who lost her key to her apartment. Attached to it is a tag with her apartment number, floor number, and door number. Brilliant! She should have just invited a thief into her home and saved him all the trouble. And so I ask you, would you ever attach your social security card, driver's license and a list of fears to your keychain? What if you lost it by accident? It all sounds like a bad idea because it *is* a bad idea.

Think of your social media profiles and technology gadgets as the exact same thing. Everything that you produce is ultimately attached to you, separate from an online handle or not. Whether it's an uploaded resume to a job bank or your personal information on a social networking site, you have to be careful about publishing personal information.

In the event that you were unknowingly being stalked or a victim of identity theft, this information in the public domain could be used to destroy you—personally and financially. Your reputation is on the line when you're online. Giving too much away up front makes it very easy for predators, bullies, and fraudsters to take advantage of your vulnerability.

Being cautious (and perhaps misleadingly mysterious) may serve you better in the long run, rather than disclosing all of your personal information online. Ultimately it is up to you to decide how personal you want to get with your social media profiles.

Exercise caution in divulging the following information:

1. *Names of your siblings.* Just because you share the same surname does not mean you have a right to introduce your siblings to the rest of the digital world.

2. *Names of your parents.* Usually your parents' names are used to verify credit card information and you may not be wise to publish their names in public sites. And, again, you may share the same blood, but not the same blog.

3. *Names of your partner and your kids.* Your own family may not be into social media sites (yet), especially your kids if they're still young. If you are keeping a personal blog, they might not want to be mentioned. Or if you really have to, stick to writing things that won't embarrass them and never use their real names.

4. *Any of your physical addresses, past or present.* Again, such information is oftentimes used for verification for bank accounts and you put yourself at risk by letting this information float around in the Web. Needless to say, you are inviting stalkers and thieves into your home by disclosing this information. You are not only putting yourself in harm's way; you are also doing the same to the people in your household.

5. *Phone numbers.* Phone numbers are sacred. This is the easiest way to get to you. Leaving this information in a job bank is understandable—but for any other reasons, why should you? If you leave your numbers in social media sites without the proper privacy settings, you can be vulnerable to telemarketing, prank calls/text messages, and other annoying situations.

6. *Identification numbers (including your Social Security number).* Identification numbers on your company ID, passport, or your driver's license are pieces of information that uniquely identify you. These numbers can also be exploited to steal your identity.

7. *Your birthday.* Again, information such as birthdays is used to verify financial transactions. Say your wallet got stolen with your credit cards. If you are on a social media site and the thief saw your birthday on it, he or she may just use it to validate a credit card transaction. Birthdays are often used by credit card companies and banks to verify cardholder identities for online or phone banking transactions.

8. *Your physical whereabouts at any one time.* Such

information attracts stalkers. Sites like Foursquare publish your whereabouts at any given time—BUT you can be proactive by showing this information to only a select few with whom you are comfortable sharing it.

9. *Your daily routine.* Sharing your daily routine may mean nothing to you but to people who are out to get you, this information is a gold mine. Knowing your habits and your whereabouts at any given time is exactly what shady characters need in order to cast a net around you. Even if you're not rich and famous, being ambushed by people you prefer not to see can happen if they know your routine.

10. *Your financial information.* This is a no-brainer. Account and PIN numbers should be kept under lock and key.

There's no such thing as a free lunch... or account

Think that Gmail, LinkedIn or Facebook account is free? Think again. Nothing is truly free!

With all of the data you voluntarily mine for them, your information is priceless. By signing up for "free" accounts, your information is essentially for sale. That includes all of your likes, dislikes, professional contacts, personal emails, and more. What price would you put on your privacy and data?

When you openly unload all of your information to a new portal or website, think about how this information can be used. Under the privacy laws in force here in the United States, every online service must disclose how they will use your information and how they will safeguard against its unlawful use.

However, despite their promises and legal enforcement, you can't possibly account for hackers or accidental transmission of information. Sometimes even hardware theft is an issue that results in an unlawful breach of privacy. Alas, hackers can always find loopholes.

Understand that even if social media sites don't disclose your personal information to others, your "free" price tag comes with display advertising, retarget marketing, unsolicited mail and other pesky things you may not necessarily welcome!

CHAPTER FIVE:
Showcasing Your Best

When you meet people face to face, you dress to impress. Online, you do the same. You impress people by the words, the colors, the images, and the sounds that you use. Learn to use these elements effectively so you can get your message across.

Email etiquette

Email is probably the mother of all other social networking platforms available today. Email, Facebook, Twitter, and LinkedIn (to name a few) all aim to connect with everyone else in the digital universe. The difference is that email remains a more personal means of correspondence.

Today, most businesses rely heavily on corresponding with clients and colleagues through email. There also seems to be an impression that you are not a professional if you do not have an email address. You get points if you have your own domain name or if your email address is that of an organization or company. Sites such as Yahoo!, Hotmail, and Google offer email services as a way of driving people to their websites. Emails and email groups build communities.

Manners and etiquette also apply to your online communications. Whether you are emailing your mother or your future boss, you will want to heed a few basic rules.

1. *Wait five minutes to send off your email.* This will allow you to proofread your email for typos and syntax and also give you time to re-read the email. Effective online communications are carefully crafted. The nature of the online world means things are published lightning fast. Take care and time to craft well thought-out emails that say exactly what you want them to say. And if you're in an office setting, treat your emails as an office memo.

2. *Never send an angry email.* If taken out of context, your reputation will be put on the line. Also, it's a really easy way to leave a negative digital footprint. Again, refer to the first point: to get your point across, actually take the time to craft your emails in a meaningful way. Hastily firing off

an email will dampen your reputation because it shows that you jump to conclusions quickly and don't take the time to think about the issue at hand.

3. *Reply or reply all?* Be sure to check whether you are replying to everyone in the email thread or to just one person. When replying to all, remember that all the recipients are privy to the information you are sending.

4. *Typos, typos, typos.* Typos in your email show that you are careless and haphazard... not exactly key building points of a relationship, professional or otherwise, right? Keep the spellcheck on to help you identify errors.

5. *Do not write in ALL CAPS.* Writing in all CAPITAL letters in an email or in any social media forum is a CAPITAL mistake. This is synonymous to shouting. Words in **bold** can have the same effect. So use both sparingly.

6. *Business email versus personal email.* Learn the difference between formatting a business email and a personal email. Always treat your office email like office memos.

7. *Keep your emails brief and to the point.* If your email is more than five sentences long it is probably too long. Keep

it brief and succinct to ensure that it is read.

8. *Respond within 24 hours of receipt.* With business emails, it is generally proper etiquette to send a reply within one day. If you are behind or backlogged, 48 hours is pushing it. Even if you are busy, send a quick acknowledgement of receipt and return to it when you have time. If you will be away for more than 48 hours (long weekends not included), make sure to use a vacation message or auto-responder to let them know that you received the email and that you will be in touch as soon as possible.

9. *"Earliest opportunity," not "earliest convenience."* One implies that you prioritize their communications. The other implies an air of entitlement and superiority. In the digital age, carefully choosing your words is everything.

10. *Respond as soon as you are able to.* There is an unwarranted notion that when people respond to emails right away it means that they don't have a life or that they have nothing else to do but sit around on the computer all day. In fact, what it shows is that you are prioritizing your communications with them and that you care enough to respond quickly. This is a very positive trait to have in your

professional life and it will serve you well to learn it early. Imagine if you sent an email off to a CEO of a major company and he got back to you within the hour. Was it because he was short on things to do that day? No—it means that he cares enough about all inquiries that pass through his desk that he will respond to them. Respond to someone as quickly as you would appreciate *your* questions or concerns to be addressed.

11. *Avoid unnecessary one-liner or one-word replies.* This can lead to email overload. A song from Barney says that *"...(Please) and thank you are the magic words"* but in emailing, not always. If you receive an email that has helped you, replying "Thank you" is just about right. However, save this word of thanks for your next long email instead. You can include that towards the end of your email—for example, *"By the way, Mike, thank you for your previous email on..."*

12. *Always use an appropriate subject line.* Emails with irrelevant subject lines will either annoy people or get ignored.

13. *Snip and quote.* When replying to an email thread, use

quotation marks when quoting someone else's text. If possible, delete the portions of the previous email/s that are no longer needed in your reply. A long thread clutters your email and may only confuse the recipient/s.

14. *Use the priority button appropriately.* Unless your email is truly urgent, do not flag your email as priority.

15. *Do not send annoying emails.* Avoid this especially when sending to business contacts. Spam, forwarded emails, hoaxes, and chain letters are all online noise that veer the recipient's focus from his work.

16. *Minimize the file size of your attachments.* When you need to attach a file into your email, make sure that you are able to compress the file size as much as you can. Remember that some company servers have a maximum allocation for email size.

17. *Put in an email signature.* Have a professional signature that lists your contact information, what you do and the best way for people to contact you, in order of preference.

18. *Read before sending.* I cannot stress strongly enough this most important rule when sending emails: read your

message again. Look out for missing words, wrong spelling or grammar, redundant words or lines, and context clarity. Your email represents you. You wouldn't want to be labeled as a bad speller or scatterbrain, would you?

Live video conferencing etiquette

Video chat is great for initial interviews and meets and greets. It may seem strange and intimidating at first but you can learn to love this form of communication by preparing for it ahead of time!

1. *Dress up for your video chat.* Try not to hold a virtual meeting in your pajamas or wrinkled clothes. Get dressed and primped just like you would for an in-person meeting or interview. At the very least, going through the motions will put you in the right mindset to treat it with the same gusto and attitude as a professional meeting.

2. *Mind your surroundings.* Try not to video conference with a bathroom or kitchen in view. Find a spot with some ambiance or create a backdrop that is conducive to a professional conversation. Maybe you want to position yourself in front of a bookcase or out on the patio with a garden behind you. Treat your video conference like you

would a photo. Remember: that's the image that the other person will remember for a while. They might even save a photo of you while they are chatting. It's always important to give a great impression, even if it is via video chat.

3. *Avoid unnecessary movements like trying to fix yourself in the monitor.* It makes you seem distracted and vain. This distracts the person you are meeting with as well.

4. *Close out all other programs and windows prior to the start of the video chat.* That way you are not distracted by flashing windows, email notifications and popup windows during an important interview or meeting.

5. *Smile.* Depending on your personality, a video conference may be more nerve-wracking than an in-person interview. If you get nervous, just smile. It will relax you a bit and help move your conversation along.

6. *Be an active listener.* It's difficult enough as it is to read body language through a video chat. Really hang on to their every word and repeat facts or inquire for more information to make sure you retain the information. Feel free to also take notes if you should so desire.

7. *Do NOT record the conversation without their permission.* It is unlawful to record, video or voice any conversation without their consent. Make sure that if you want to record the conversation, you have a good reason for doing so and that you can do it without interrupting the conversation.

Blogs and public forums

Depending on how they are used, blogs and public forums can either help you build or destroy your professional and personal presence online. It all depends on the content and purpose for which you are writing. Blogs are powerful things!

Writing your blog

It's fairly easy to do and it's free. Just choose one from the major blogging platforms, like WordPress. If you need some topics try starting with:

1. Something related to your field of interest or expertise

2. A reaction to a piece of recent news

3. A piece on your inspiration or motivation

4. Something about someone you admire

5. Some great advice that was recently imparted upon you

6. An interesting experience you've had

7. Places you have visited.

Try not to write anything that may jeopardize you in any way later on. Remember, the power of the digital footprint can outlive your job search and haunt you after you've been hired! Every now and then, review the things you've published in your blog and edit or delete as needed.

Here are some tips that might help you write an effective blog post:

1. *Leave posting of news and press releases to the press.* Your blog is meant to be your personal take on a topic. Instead of echoing what already is a hot topic, share your insights and opinions on it. Sharing your learning and reflections is what incites people to read what you have to say.

2. *Blog regularly.* It doesn't mean you have to write daily. Stick to a schedule you can commit to. Whether it is once or twice a week, having a schedule will help discipline you.

This way your readers know when to expect a new post from you as well.

3. *Elicit comments.* Make sure your comment feature is up and running. Your blog post should be a way to connect with your readers. If they comment or leave a message on your blog, be sure to answer back.

4. *Some commentary (yours and your readers') may become a hot topic.* Be prepared to police the comments posted as well. Delete as needed what may be offensive and libelous. Better yet, you can opt to check a reader's comment before allowing it to be published on your blog.

5. *Make your blog visible.* No, you don't have to hire someone to do SEO programming on your blog. Make use of what is available to you. You can tweet about a new blog post or publish in Facebook. Use words that are search-friendly and use an RSS feed. Another way is to ask friends with blogs to include your link in their blogroll—and of course you must do the same for them.

6. *Keep it real.* Don't post something that you can't say face to face. It is annoying to read an arrogant post by a blogger who hasn't the guts to say the same in person.

7. If you want to spruce up your blog, there are ready-made templates you can choose from. Once you have gotten comfortable blogging, you can move on to personalizing your blog the way you want.

Commenting on blogs

Commenting allows you to connect with the author of a blog post and to the other readers. More often than not, you glean more information this way. Another by-product of commenting is that when "searchable" useful information is posted, you get more "hits" in your site. To keep a good flow of discussion going in the comment section, whether in your blog or another person's, it's best to keep the following in mind:

1. *Be brief (as much as possible).* I understand that some hot topics tend to elicit really long replies. However, if you can be brief, I'm sure the other readers will appreciate it. If you want to add more, you can put in a link to where you got the additional information. If you really feel strongly about the topic, it would be good to write about it in your own site and put a pingback or link (refer to the blog post that pushed you to express

your opinion).

2. *Zone in on what struck a chord.* Comment on what caught your attention in a blog post or a previous comment. Be as specific as you can. It's good to hear that you found the post helpful, but do try to add your own thoughts. If you need to quote, quote away but sparingly. You don't want to be quoting the whole blog post, do you?

3. *A click on the "Like" button goes a long way.* Bloggers write their heart out, baring their souls to their audience. So, if you can't leave a whole lot of comment, clicking on the "Like" button is more than enough.

4. *Don't promote your own blog or website.* When commenting, there is a field you have to fill out that includes your inputting of a link to your own site. Your username already automatically links you to your site. So there is no need for you to say in your comment, *"Hey, by the way, visit my site too at http://www.somesite.com."*

5. *Be on track.* Stick to the topic at hand. Remember that if you veer too far from the topic, your comment can be

deleted by the blog owner.

6. *Be polite.* With so many people speaking their mind, I'm sure you won't be agreeing with all the comments. There is ALWAYS a good way of saying things. Always put yourself on the receiving end when writing your comment. How would that person feel reading what you have to say?

Status updates

Getting clicker-happy on Twitter, Facebook or Foursquare? Someone will notice... and, if you ever have a TMI (too much information) moment, immediately delete it. Even if you think just for a second that it might be inappropriate or that it might come back and haunt you, it is better to erase it quickly than to have it catch up with you later.

Try not to give a play by play of your daily life, either. Be very cautious of updating your status with your location or other information that may compromise your safety. Sometimes giving too much information does not leave a lot to the imagination. If someone knows your every thought and movement, it is not necessary to get to know you! Don't go overboard with the updates. Learn to be a little mysterious.

Photos & videos

Be mindful of photo and video updates. Make sure that they are appropriate for all audiences. Steer away from photos with beers, alcohol, cigarettes, drugs etc. Also try not to post photos when you play hooky (because you will eventually do that). There are tons of horror stories of people who called in a sick day and then posted a photo or status update of them on the beach. It's a great way to get fired!

Videos are a tricky thing, too: try to show your best side. Post videos of you doing smart and intelligent things, not silly things. Maybe you have a friend tape a speech you made in class or running an experiment in the lab. Maybe a group of your friends go to a charity event and you snag some interviews with the VIPs. Those are great videos that show the world what you want to be remembered for. Leave the videos of you in Cancun on the beach at home.

CHAPTER SIX:
Sticky Situations and How To Deal

Cyberstalking and cyberbullying

Cyberstalking and cyberbullying are acts that usually go together. It is a scary, real, and unfortunate truth that we have to deal with. At some point in your digital life you will come across a statement or action that will make you feel uncomfortable. It may be annoying or downright hostile. The mistake that people make is that they believe they cannot be prosecuted for crimes or harassment committed through a virtual space. Know that they are wrong and that you may take steps to combat it. A number of students have chosen to ignore harassment and it has led to some deadly results.

Studies show that cyberbullying and cyberstalking are widespread, affecting not only the U.S. but European and Eastern countries as well. Mostly affected are the pre-teens and teenagers.

Cyberbullying happens everywhere. Cyberbullying does not choose any race or culture.

Defense against cyberbullying and cyberstalking

The first step to dealing with this is educating yourself on harassment, the causes thereof, and how to manage the conflict yourself and by enlisting the help of others.

1. *Contact the police.* If you feel that you are in true danger, contact your local law enforcers immediately. You should do so especially if you believe that your cyberstalker knows your actual physical location. Take steps to ensure your safety.

2. *Save all digital communications.* Keeping diligent records will give you a basis from which to understand what is happening and the best steps to take. Such information is evidence that can be used to file a valid complaint against your cyberstalker.

3. *Address the perpetrator in a calm, professional, and matter-of-fact tone.* Tell them that you do not want to receive any form of communications from them. Let them know that you will turn them in to the appropriate

authorities if they attempt to contact you again.

4. *Whenever you can block or ignore a cyberbully, do so.* The best way to dissipate a one-sided argument is to check out of it altogether. If the cyberbully is on Facebook, unfriend him/her and block him/her out.

5. *Do not retaliate.* Fighting fire with fire will only exacerbate the problem. Try to stay calm even if you are flustered and scared.

6. *Let other people know what is going on.* Tell your friends, parents, boss, the dean of your college, the police, etc. As an adult, there are hopefully less challenges in admitting when someone is threatening your wellbeing and safety. You deserve the rally of support you will receive to fend against the culprit.

7. *Carefully manage your privacy settings on your social networking profiles and personal websites.* Opt to keep your information exclusive to a select group of friends and family you trust implicitly. Consider going off the grid altogether for a while.

8. *Enlist the help of your Internet service provider to block*

the messages if you are receiving threatening or harassing emails. You can forward your messages to postmaster@yourispwebaddress.com and explain your situation. You can also call customer service so that they may note your account and notify authorities on your behalf and work with the technical support staff to attempt email-specific blocking.

9. *If you are receiving threatening calls to your personal cell phone, keep the number in service to capture and timestamp every attempt they make to get in touch with you.* Save all messages, text messages, picture messages, and call logs so that you can build a case. When you have quantitative proof, it is much more difficult to dismiss your concerns as paranoia. Get a prepaid cellular phone for use within your immediate group of friends and family. When you inform them of your new phone number, make sure you let them know that you have been having issues with cyberstalking or harassment and to safeguard your information.

10. If you have reason to believe that your personal and financial information is at risk, put a security hold on your

information at the three national credit bureaus.

11. If you are receiving threatening messages through your social media profile, contact them so that they may help stop the abuse. Chances are the attacker is using the site in violation of the terms of service and can be subjected to account cancellation or legal action.

12. In the event that the accused is geographically close to you—as in, they are a classmate, dorm mate, old coworker or a bitter ex, file a temporary restraining order in the city in which the first offense occurred. During the period between its issuance date and your court date, gather all of the evidence you compiled in the above steps to receive a permanent restraining order. If you feel unsafe confronting the accused, you may send a lawyer to take care of the matter on your behalf.

Sadly, cyberbullying is something that happens all the time. For more information on cyberbullying and actions to take, you may refer to the following:

• Center for Safe and Responsible Internet Use (http://www.cyberbully.org)

- Cyberbullying Research Center
  (http://www.cyberbully.us/)

Slander and libel

Slander is any communication that reports a false and malicious statement about someone and attacks their reputation. Libel is the act of printing or publishing a statement for the purposes of defaming a living person. With issues concerning slander or libel online, an ounce of prevention is really worth a pound of cure. It is much easier to manage the damage to your reputation online sooner than later. Quick and swift action is necessary since many people who search for something on Google perceive the first page of results as factual.

Defense against slander and libel

When slander and libel is escalated and becomes more serious and a threat to your personal safety, follow the steps in *Cyberbullying and Cyberstalking* to protect yourself. It is always better to be safe than sorry. When culprits can hide behind the "safety" of a computer screen or their keyboard, you are only enabling them by not working through the issue with the appropriate authorities. Stop cyber crimes and end the victimization cycle.

1. Request that your content be removed from websites. You can generally contact the site owner directly to remove libelous statements.

2. Contrary to popular belief, major search engines do not publish your information. They just report information that is publicly accessible on the Internet. You can request that URLs (Web addresses) be removed if they accidentally expose personal information.

3. It is easier to bury information than it is to get it erased. Create fresh and new content under your name to begin bumping up positive content and burying negative content. You can do this quite easily with WordPress, Twitter, and LinkedIn.

4. If the comments are inextricably linked to your profile or account, deactivate the account and start a new one on a clean slate. Make sure to block the culprit or they will just repeat their behavior.

5. Be proactive, not reactive. Address the perpetrator but do not react to his/her actions. Send your request together with a cease-and-desist letter outlining what they've done by showing a timeline. Never ignore their actions. In fact,

you should track every time they slander your reputation --- keep record! However, reacting or responding negatively to the perpetrator's actions will only add fuel to their fire and motivate them to continue.

6. Never confront or agree to meet the slanderer in person. You may put yourself in grave danger and invite new, future or continued attacks. Or if you feel that talking to the person will help stop the issue, best to bring with you a friend or family member, legal adviser, and the authority if needed.

Be careful how you lash out on the Web.

Risks to employment

Social media and technology can be fun, but how far will you take it? There are horror stories of people posting status updates to their Twitter and getting fired before lunch. There was even a story of a young woman who had her job offer rescinded because of information her new employer was able to dig up on her online. Again, the recurring theme here is to responsibly manage your online presence and your communications.

The bottom line is to not give anyone any ammunition to use against you, in the workplace or otherwise. Adding your boss or co-employee as a friend to your Facebook account may not be wise. Use technology in your favor to shine a positive light on your image and get ahead. Don't let your social media profiles hold you in the past!

Here are some things that can get you pretty much terminated immediately (or at the very least bullied out of your job):

1. *Leaking confidential company information.* This is a strict NO-NO in every industry, whether it's your advertising agency's newest campaign in the works or your research team's new vaccine in development. Leaking confidential company information can be a breach of contract depending on your employment agreement. It can also subject you to fines, penalties, and legal implications under trademark, copyright, and intellectual property laws. Be cautious of anything you post about work. Be extra cautious if you have the slightest inclination of hesitation. In the case of confidentiality, it is better to adamantly withhold information than to deal with the massive backlash if you leak.

2. *Publicly posting recommendations and quotes without permission.* This is a touchy subject for many. To be safe, I would consider no email, text, wall post, tweet or otherwise electronic communication to ever be held in any sort of private confidence. Get into the habit of asking for recommendations that speak to a very specific event, task, or project.

3. *Employer invasion of privacy.* Laws are rapidly shifting and changing. Never assume anything online is private and you will avoid later heartache. If you want to keep something private, keep it to yourself!

4. *Termination of your employment because of off-hours conduct and legal recreational activities.* The laws vary from state to state so you will have to consult with an attorney if you want to pursue legal avenues. Also take a step back and re-examine the situation in terms of whether you want to work for an employer who reacts this dramatically to something you posted online in your free time. This might be a blessing in disguise!

5. Before posting a photo of yourself, check if you are wearing anything that may connect you with your employer.

Wearing a slightly unbuttoned office uniform and then posing for the camera in a "come hither" fashion is not something your employer will look at kindly. For them, you are still representing their company and your photos might ruin their reputation.

6. *FTC regulations on company endorsements.* If you work in advertising, marketing, or PR it is important to be mindful of what you post on company social media profiles, blogs, forums, and the like. Your company can be held liable for endorsements and misleading statements posted by an employee in which the employment relationship is not disclosed.

What to do in the case of mistaken identity

Do your due diligence before you take interviews with potential employers. Dig up information on yourself (refer to chapter 2) before thinking about sending out your resume or link to a potential employer. If you find that someone is impersonating you or posting libelous statements that are damaging to your online reputation, take steps to protect yourself by referring to the relevant sections in this book.

Identity theft is a serious problem, and as the digital divide continues to widen, it is important to take these matters into your own hands before the security system can catch up with the complexity of the crimes committed. Doing nothing about identity theft can affect your ability to buy a car, rent a house or apartment, get a job, apply for insurance, get a cell phone, and even rent movies at a local video store. This is your future so do everything you can to protect it!

Regaining control

If you are a victim of identity theft, there are steps you can take to clear your public records. Above all else:

1. Keep diligent records.

2. Follow up with everyone you get in touch with.

3. Do not pay any bill or portion thereof that is a result of fraud.

Stay calm and do not allow yourself to be forced into paying fraudulent bills. Notify the three national credit bureaus and establish a fraud alert on your file. Generally, calling one alerts all three but you might want to cross-check just in case. This alert is only good for 90 days but during this time you can call them back and request an extension of up to seven years.

Equifax

P.O. Box 740250, Atlanta, GA 30374- 0241.

Report fraud: Call (888) 766-0008

TDD: (800) 255-0056

www.equifax.com

Experian

PO Box 9532 Allen TX, 75013

Report fraud: Call (888) EXPERIAN or

(888-397-3742)

TDD: Use relay to fraud number above.

www.experian.com/fraud

TransUnion

P.O. Box 6790, Fullerton, CA 92834-6790.

Report fraud: (800) 680-7289

TDD: (877) 553-7803

Email (fraud victims only): fvad@transunion.com

www.transunion.com

1.   *Request multiple copies of your credit report and review*

them carefully. That way you can report fraudulent activity promptly and begin the process of clearing your name. It is important to be diligent and to have written, recorded, and physical evidence of your notifications. Make sure you follow their protocol to ensure that your public records are cleared up. Failing to follow their directions will result in delays and the situation might be more difficult for you to handle later on.

2. *File reports with your local police station.* If you have legal documentation of fraud, the credit bureaus will be able to better determine if they can remove reports from your records. In the state of California this is the law. The more written documentation you have, the better.

3. *File reports with the Federal Trade Commission.* Although they cannot investigate your claims, they will be able to share this information with other agencies that manage these problems for other groups of people.

4. *Learn the Victim's Statement of Rights under federal law at www.idtheft.gov.* If fraudulent accounts have been opened under your name, notify the relevant banks and creditors immediately in writing and by telephone. Make

sure to have fraud affidavits filled out and ready to submit
when you make the call (you can download and use a stock
FTC version at
http://www.ftc.gov/bcp/edu/resources/forms/affidavit.pd
f). Provide as many detailed reports as you can that will
help them clear up this problem.

5. *If you have current accounts that have been compromised,
   reset all of your account numbers by requesting new
   cards and new accounts as applicable.* Chances are the
   companies you are currently doing business with will be
   more than happy to help you. In helping you they also
   prevent themselves from losing money as well.

6. *Are you now receiving debt collection calls?* The agents are
   generally very rude, will speak very quickly to confuse you,
   using scare tactics to verbally beat you into a payment. Be
   calm, matter of fact, and explain that they purchased bad
   debt that resulted from identity theft. Document the name
   and employee number of any and all agents that call you.
   Also ask them to furnish information on which creditor
   they purchased the debt from so that you can also get in
   touch with that company and explain your situation. Offer

a fraud affidavit and be diligent in following up with them to ensure they received the information they require and that the account has been closed or otherwise taken care of.

7. *If you are a victim of fraud in banking (checking accounts and savings accounts), your bank should provide you with an affidavit and discuss with you all of the charges, pending and processed.* When dealing with identity theft, loss of money from your checking and savings accounts is definitely more devastating because it can take quite a while for the money to be returned to you. (When it's credit fraud, it's not your money, just your reputation.) After you file the necessary paperwork with your bank, make sure to contact the check verification systems to also notify them of fraud.

Fidelity National Information Services

(800) 437-5120 www.fidelityinfoservices.com

SCAN

(800) 262-7771 www.consumerdebit.com

TeleCheck

(800) 366-2425, (800) 835-3243, or (800) 710-9898

www.telecheck.com

CrossCheck

(800) 843-0760 www.cross-check.com

Other types of fraud

1. *Fraud involving your brokerage accounts (IRAs, stocks, etc)*. Report the incident directly to your brokerage firm and provide them with all of the documentation they require to attempt recovery of your funds. Notify the SEC (Securities Exchange Commission) and the Financial Industry Regulation Association.

2. *Postal service fraud*. Speak with your mail carrier and your local postal inspector by calling 1-800-275-8777. You may also file a complaint at https://postalinspectors.usps.gov.

3. *Social Security fraud*. If your Social Security number has been misused, call their hotline (800) 269-0271 for further instructions. They recommend against changing the number unless it is a very serious case of fraud.

4. *Passport fraud*. Get in touch with your local passport office (usually at the US Postal Service offices). Learn more at http://www.travel.state.gov/passport/lost/lost_849.html

5. *Medical identity theft.* If you are a victim of medical identity theft and false civil and criminal judgments, you will definitely want to enlist the help of an attorney and law enforcement to handle the matter and advise you on the next steps.

Immediate damage control

So you've just sent a not-so-nice note to the entire office thanks to "Reply All," or you got caught red-handed violating etiquette protocol or company policy. How will you deal with the embarrassment and backlash? There are ways to do it with grace and hopefully recoup any lost credibility. Despite your best intentions, you will eventually slip up. Although it will take some time to get back to where you were before, these tips may help you address this situation with class and repair your reputation.

What is the best way to deal with it?

1. *Own up to your mistake.* Accept fault when you make a mistake. That may include making a formal apology to one person or many, depending on what you did. Genuinely apologize for any inconvenience this may have caused them.

2. *Address the mistake.* Depending if you offended one person or many, address the mistake in an open and honest environment. If you accidentally slammed a coworker, take him/her aside privately and openly apologize and explain yourself. If you slammed your entire office in a mistake email, a public apology may be in order.

3. *Offer a promise to not repeat said mistake.* Sometimes this is not possible, especially in the case that you slam your entire office and you get fired. However, if you only managed to anger one or two people, it's best to promise to be on your best behavior from here on forward.

4. *Maintain a positive attitude despite the atmosphere.* It's not unreasonable to deal with an uncomfortable atmosphere for a while—a day or maybe a week at most. Such issues generally work themselves out in a short timeframe. However, if things are still awkward after a week, it might be best to move on, whether it is a friend or a workplace. People who hold grudges are no fun to be around and can spread the toxicity to others.

5. *Stay positive and plot your next move.* Just make sure you are gracious every step of the way.

Depending on the severity of your mistake, prepare for possible litigation. You may want to consult with lawyers regarding libel and slander if the problem won't go away or if you face any sort of major retaliation or sabotage.

CHAPTER SEVEN:
Marrying Your Online and Offline Lives

Your sometimes online life will increasingly encroach on your real day-to-day life. Like all relationships, this marriage will take work and devotion. Ensuring that you take the time to carefully craft your online persona with the same gusto and verve you take to craft yourself in real life will ensure a seamless marriage and turn your two lives into one!

It is important to have your online self truly represent who you are in real life. As semantic Web technology takes hold of the Internet in Web 3.0 and transforms our digital experience for the next few years, you need to be prepared to face yourself in multiple digital mediums.

If people cannot find you online right now, they will assume that you are in the dark about technology or that you do not exist. Of course you will exist in person. The problem is that you will have no digital footprint.

In the age of the Internet, not having a digital footprint is the same as not existing at all. It is better to begin establishing your online presence now. You can organically grow it as you go, rather than waiting for someone else to do it for you unwillingly and tarnish your good name before you're even in the game.

Integrating your multiple lives isn't terribly difficult. Know yourself and stay true to your voice. Don't try to be someone else (figuratively and literally). Just be yourself and keep your messages in check!

Consistency is the key

There are a lot of social media sites out there and I'm sure you didn't sign up for only one. Chances are, you are active in two or more. The people closest to me are users of Facebook, Twitter, LinkedIn, and maintain a blog as well. You can say that they are very sociable people.

When engaging in a number of social media sites, make sure that your online persona is consistent in each one. How you "sound" on

Facebook should be the same for Twitter, your blog, and everything else. Seamlessly translate your offline style to your online style. This way you are able to show your true self even on the Web. Having multiple personalities may be fun but sooner or later it will wear you out. Your audience or the people you interact with online will lose interest.

Consistently post information worth reading. When posting, ask yourself, "Is this some information I'd like to read from somebody else?" If not, then do not post at all! I don't know about you but some people give TOO MUCH INFORMATION that nobody really cares about. Don't be that person. Such people sometimes come across as being too needy for attention. Don't forget that your online life is not the totality of who you are. Get off that chair and live your life!

Cross-linking

All cross-linking entails is having your information connected through a central portal. Say you start a personal website that features your blog and you want the public at large to be able to access you on Facebook, Twitter, LinkedIn, YouTube, and elsewhere. Cross-linking allows them to simply click on a graphic or linked text and be redirected to your social media profiles.

If you have a blog, it would be good to post links to sites that you actively participate in.

Cross-posting

If you don't want to bother with maintaining different social media profiles and websites, you can automate it! It is possible to have information cross-fed into your other channels if you link them together. This way you won't need to update your Twitter and Facebook accounts at the same time. You can automatically have it post your update to both platforms. Here's how you can do it with popular social media sites:

1. Twitter to your website:

   http://twitter.com/goodies/widgets

2. Twitter to Facebook:

   https://twitter.com/about/resources/widgets/facebook

3. Twitter to LinkedIn: http://learn.linkedin.com/twitter/

4. Facebook to your website:

   http://www.networkedblogs.com/

5. Facebook to Twitter: http://apps.facebook.com/twitter/

6. Smartphone to Twitter: http://m.twitter.com

7. Smartphone to Facebook: http://facebook.com/mobile

8. Smartphone to YouTube:
    http://www.youtube.com/mobile

9. YouTube to Twitter: Share or Embed button on your
    video's page, learn more at
    http://www.youtube.com/youtubeonyoursite

10. Youtube to Facebook: Share or Embed button on your
    video's page, learn more at
    http://www.youtube.com/youtubeonyoursite

11. Youtube to your website:
    http://www.youtube.com/youtubeonyoursite

"Friending" your coworkers and bosses online

Getting to know people in your organization is encouraged. It will
not only help you understand your company's culture but also help
you in your quest to move up or across the career ladder. Getting
to know someone is one thing, but getting friendly with them

online is a different animal altogether!

Chances are when you are first hired to work at a new company, you will be on your best behavior for the first ninety days. That is the general probationary period during which you are concentrating on knocking off the socks of your department and supervisor. It is probably for the best to keep your focus on impressing them and doing good work, and not befriending them online.

It is recommended that you stay "off the grid" during this probationary period and limit your exposure. These first ninety days will help you set the precedence for the rest of your time with the company. Use the first ninety days to do some general housekeeping: lock your profile, delete or hide photos, clean up offensive posts. Maybe someone in HR didn't do that thorough of a background check on you. It is probably best that they never get to dig up dirt on you during your first ninety days!

Maybe by the halfway mark you will have fostered some great working relationships. If you're at a small company, that is highly likely. Even if you receive friend requests, hold off on accepting them. Some people will wonder what's going on and might contact you. Use this opportunity to let them know that you have been focusing on your work and career endeavors and simply haven't had the chance to sign on yet. On day ninety (preferably after you've accepted your new employment agreement), go ahead and friend them and put everything you've learned about managing social media and technology into practice.

Have the essentials on hand

The beauty of going digital is that you don't have to be bringing a bunch of papers everywhere you go. You can just have everything in a memory stick and print the essentials as needed. It is imperative that you have important documents about you within easy reach all the time. Also, don't forget to have a backup copy of all your digital copies somewhere safe. Use a password key as well for your confidential files. Have the following information in digital format:

1. *Virtual business card.* You can set it up using Address Book (Mac) or Outlook (PC). Save the *.vcf file with your name, email address, avatar, Web address, phone number, and other pertinent information.

2. *Decent headshot.* You don't need to get it professionally

done (it would be nice though!) but just have something on hand that is presentable in case someone at work needs to use your image somewhere. As with the video conference, be aware of your backdrop!

3. *Updated resume and work portfolio.* Keep it updated and include all of the new skills you have acquired and are acquiring at your new job.

4. *Scans of your legal documents.* If you lose your ID, passport, or birth certificate, it will be helpful to have a digital set while you are waiting for a replacement. For security purposes, password-lock these files to safeguard against unauthorized viewing.

5. *Insurance paperwork.* Scan and keep digital files of your auto, health, life, liability, and disability insurance.

6. *Medical records.* Keep scanned records of everything you have from your general practitioner, specialists, vision care, dental care, etc. Have a list of your current medications, over-the-counter or otherwise. Also have your doctor's information scanned in just in case someone else in your family needs to speak on your

behalf.

7. *Academic records.* Keep scans of your degree, transcripts, diploma, and certificates.

8. *Work records.* If you have any paperwork you received from your employer, scan it as well.

CHAPTER EIGHT:
Putting Your New Social Media Skills to Good Use

As you now know, there are a lot of uses for social media. While some people are oversharing their personal thoughts and feelings, you now know better. The question still remains, though: How will you put social media to good use?

There are many ways to use social media to find a job, connect with like-minded friends, meet new people, and dig for information. The Internet is a digital wellspring of wealth, knowledge, and contributors. All you have to do is set yourself up and you're ready to make a dent in a relatively large parallel universe.

A lot of the fundamentals of interpersonal communications still remain, though. The Internet isn't a substitute for interactions that foster deep relationships. It is a place where you can harvest a lot of information, both pertinent and erroneous. It is also a place where giving is just as rewarding as receiving. You will find an entanglement of people who are friendly and willing to help, along with people with ulterior motives.

Getting comfortable with technology is an absolute necessity in today's world. The Internet is not a trend – it is the wave of the future. It is never too late to get started. It can be overwhelming at times, but as with anything in life, it is important to keep forging your path and absorbing as much as you can. With the knowledge you have gained from reading this book, you can put your newfound social media skills to good use.

Starting your own business

Having started my own design and marketing business, I learned a lot of the following lessons firsthand. This entire section could be a book in its own right. However, here are some of the most crucial points that can help you utilize social media efficiently when embarking on the journey of starting your own business.

1. You can set up a new website with all of your business information. Your potential customers can access this information 24 hours a day. It can serve as a storefront for your business when you are unavailable and can answer

questions about your services or mission.

2. You can set up a blog that demonstrates your expertise. You can set up a writing schedule for sharing valuable information about the work that you do. That way, when potential customers visit your blog, they will feel comfortable knowing that you know the ins and outs of your business.

3. You can set up a professional profile on LinkedIn and connect with old coworkers, bosses, and classmates. They can provide endorsements or references, and in a roundabout way legitimize your experience.

4. You can set up any preferential social network account and begin connecting with like-minded folks. You can also use these social media connections to maintain a pulse on industry-specific news.

5. Explore advertising and marketing channels outside of the main social networks. Use your established social media profiles to help direct people to information they need, right when they need it.

6. Always link to your social media profiles from your email

signature, business cards, billing statements, marketing materials, etc.

7. Quickly respond to messages when someone reaches out to you electronically. When you respond quickly, you give the impression that you care and are responsible. When you are first establishing your business this is incredibly important. If you are eager, then eagerly respond to emails. If you wait 24-48 hours (or even longer) you may come off as irresponsible or lazy.

8. Learn how to automate as much as you can. This is especially important since responding to messages can be a full time job all by itself. When you update your blog, it can post a status update to Facebook, Twitter, and Tumblr. When you update your LinkedIn, it can notify all of your followers and friends on Twitter and Facebook. When you write a blog post, you can send an email notification, tweet, or LinkedIn status update. Reference how this is done or look it up online. That way, at the push of a button, you can update multiple statuses at the same time. Another thing to consider automating is your email. You can set up an auto responder when you are away, so that people know when to

expect a live response from you. You can also look for tools to automate email marketing campaigns. The possibilities are endless!

Looking for a new job

I've also had the pleasure of looking for work online. This includes work as a freelancer/contractor and as a full-time employee. I've also hired people online based on their profiles and their online personas. There are quite a few things to consider when it comes to your social media profiles when looking for a new job.

1. Keep your information up to date. Does your profile still mention your old company, or does it actively state that you're on the hunt for a new position? Be precise and clear about your intent. Don't aim for a generic profile unless you are looking to be passed over (or if you are looking for a similarly generic response).

2. Update your resume and upload a portfolio of work to LinkedIn. This is important nowadays since recruiters spend less than ten seconds on a LinkedIn profile before passing it over for another.

3. Make sure that you thoroughly "sanitize" your online

profiles. Delete any status updates, posts, or photos that may seem offensive to someone. Remember, anything you post can end up working against you in the job hunt. You don't want to give anyone a reason not to like you at this stage of the game.

4. Update your information regularly. You can literally stay at the top of someone's timeline if you update your information enough on Facebook, Twitter, or LinkedIn. Whenever you update or post any information, these services will create reminder updates to the people you are connected to, informing them that you've made these updates. Most of the time, people are curious enough to click through. When you do this, you not only give the impression that your information is up to date, but you also stay in the forefront of people's minds. This is the age-old game of "impressions." In advertising, companies pay very good money to increase the number of impressions, or times that their content is put in front of somebody. It generally takes seven or more impressions before someone takes action with the information in front of them, so when it comes to the job hunt this is very important.

5. Create or maintain a blog. Keep it as professional as possible. Even if you don't create new content or entries, you can always post news snippets of the day or write a quick opinion on what is going on with your industry. The objective of a blog isn't to suddenly make you do extra work for no reason, but rather to give recruiters and employers a destination site where they can learn even more about the person you are and how well you understand the industry you're in. This may give you a competitive edge in the marketplace.

6. Regularly check your messages. This one is incredibly important. I was guilty of missing a few messages–some by almost a week—and I almost missed out on some great opportunities because of it!

7. Fill out as much information as you can. Try not to leave any part of your profile blank. Let the Internet do its work for you and help drive traffic to your profile or website. The more content you put out there, the more ways people will be able to find you. Just make sure you are ready for them when they click through to learn more about who you are!

LAST WORD

Your digital self is only a glimpse of who you truly are as a person. However, in this era in which we rely heavily on digital networking, your online persona is the representation most visible to people everywhere. Make social networking work for you. Build your online presence by showcasing yourself at your very best. Take advantage of the platforms that are available. Lastly, participate actively in the public forums and stick to proper etiquette. If you do so, you'll have one fantastic life—whether online or offline.

ABOUT THE AUTHOR

As a designer and marketer, Amara has taken her skills to businesses and organizations around the world. She is passionate about startups and helping bridge the gap between technology and its users. Her specialties include User Experience Design, Visual Graphic Design, and Marketing Communications. When not working on design and marketing projects, Amara can be found volunteering for charities, training for endurance events, and blogging at http://ironwomanintraining.com.